ESSENTIAL

# Yoga

hinkler

This book is dedicated to the memory of Hunter, who taught me
about unconditional love and how to enjoy life every day.

Special thanks to my partner and best friend, Kent, for his amazing support and inspiration, his encouragement
to aim for the stars, and his belief that anything is possible.

Gena Kenny

Author: Gena Kenny
Editor: Kate Cuthbert
Art Director: Paul Scott
Photography: Ned Meldrum
Cover design: Sam Grimmer
Prepress: Graphic Print Group

All clothing provided by Lululemon, Melbourne Australia

All Leza Lowitz quotes from *Yoga: Lines to Unfold By*,
author Leza Lowitz, Stone Bridge Press, 2000

Thanks to Rosemary and Robert Ungar

# hinkler

First published in 2008
by Hinkler Books Pty Ltd
45–55 Fairchild Street
Heatherton Victoria 3202 Australia
www.hinklerbooks.com

Text © Hinkler Books Pty Ltd 2008
Design © 2008, 2011, 2014, 2016

Sunset in Himalaya © Dmitryp/Dreamstime.com
Sunset silhouette © Shaiksweet/Dreamstime.com
Beach abstract © Paul Morley/Dreamstime.com
Beach stones © Yulia Saponova/Dreamstime.com
Beach shoreline close-up © Gvision/Dreamstime.com

Decorative page motifs, chapter openers
and packaging pattern © Natasha R Graham/Dreamstime.com

All rights reserved.

No part of this publication may be utilised in any form or by any means electronic
or mechanical, including photocopying, recording or by any information storage or
retrieval system now known or hereafter invented, without the prior written permission
of the publishers.

Printed and bound in China

ISBN 978 1 4889 2950 2

Always do the warm-up exercises before attempting any individual exercises. It is
recommended that you check with your doctor or healthcare professional before
commencing any exercise regime. While every care has been taken in the preparation
of this material, the publishers and their respective employees or agents will not accept
responsibility for injury or damage occasioned to any tperson as a result of
participation in the activities described in this book.

# Contents

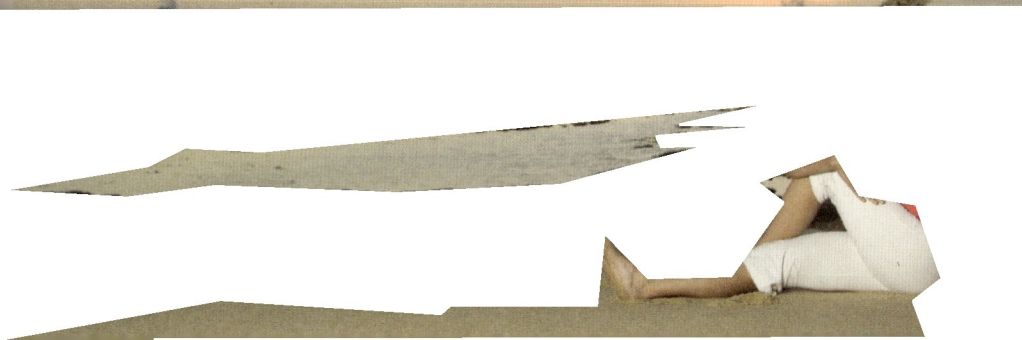

**Introduction**   5
Postures, Breath, Relaxation

**About Yoga**   8
Benefits of Yoga, Principles of Postures, Surrender/Letting go, Grounding, Alignment, Breath

**Preparing to Practise**   13
Create your Space, Prepare your Body and Mind, Yoga Tools

**Workouts**   15
Energising, Strengthening, Flexibility, Relaxation

**Warm up**   17
Mountain, Arm and Shoulder Warming, Butterfly Hands, Spinal Warming, Head Tilts/Neck Stretch, Lateral Stretch, Standing Gentle Spinal Twist, Elephant, Standing Forward Bend, Spinal Rolls, Standing Cat, Standing Chest Opener

**Sun Salutations**   27
Sun Salutations Sequence

**Standing postures**   34
Warrior 2, Extended Warrior, Dancing Warrior, Triangle

**Balances**   39
Toes/Heels Combo, Tree, Dancer, Eagle, Transitional Sequence

**Backward bends**   44
Locust, Half Bow, Bow, Extended Puppy, Upwards Dog, Half Bridge, Dynamic Half Bridge, Knee-Hug and Rock, Happy Baby

**Forward bends**   51
Forward Bend Sequence

**Spinal Twists**   54
Seated Spinal Twist, Rolling Spinal Twist, Lying Spinal Twist

**Relaxation & Meditation**   58
Meditation, Aids to Meditation or Relaxation

**Conclusion**   62

**Glossary**   63

**About the author**   64

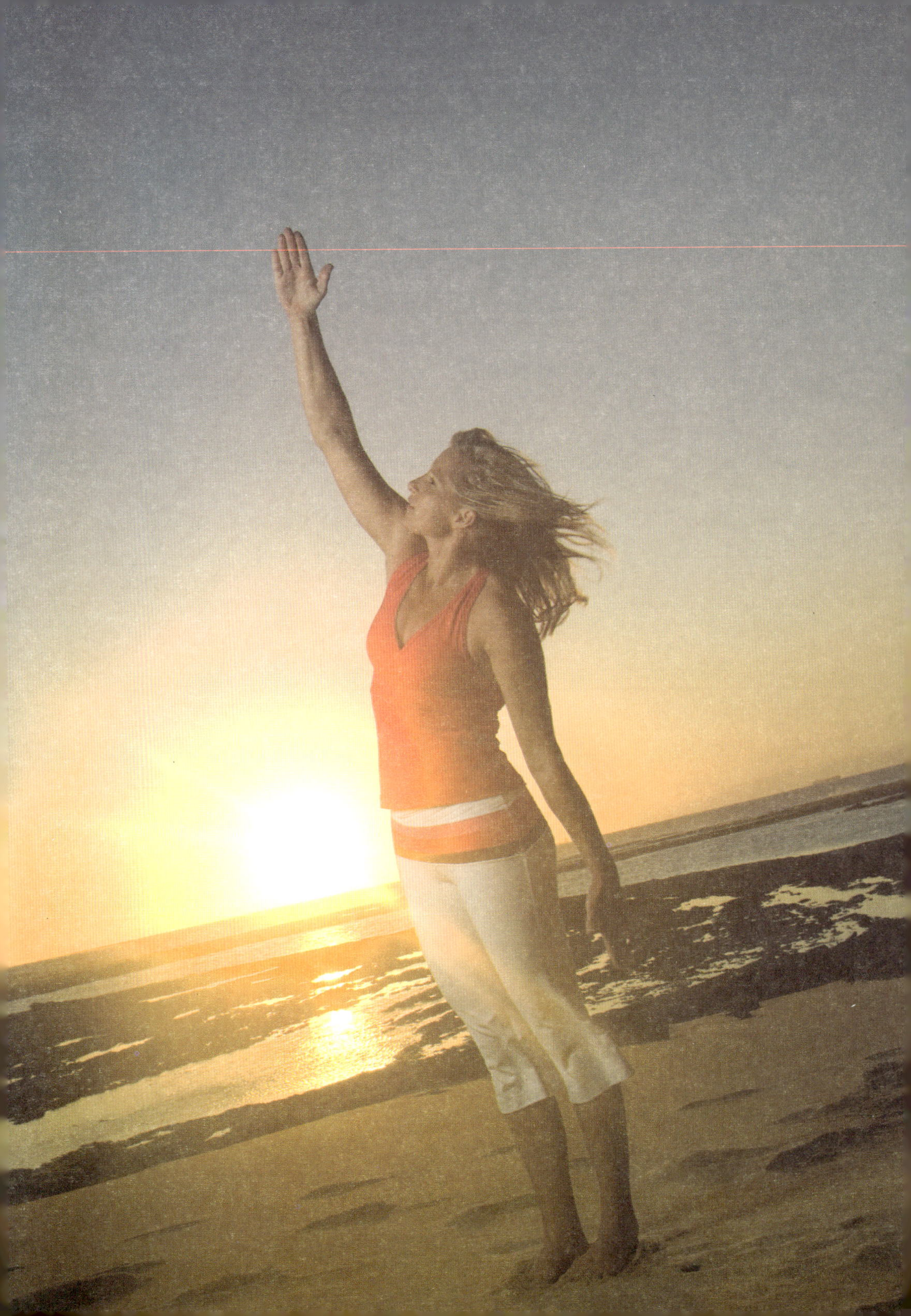

*Introduction*

# INTRODUCTION

*Good for the body is the work of the body, good for the soul is the work of the soul, and good for either is the work of the other.*

*— Henry David Thoreau*

Welcome to *Essential Yoga*. In the pages of this book, I will share with you the principles of self discovery and ways to develop a deeper understanding of your physical, emotional and mental state of being. Whether you are just beginning your journey into yoga or have been practising yoga for years, I hope you will gain valuable knowledge and, most importantly, enjoyment and fulfilment through your yoga practice.

Yoga teaches us to reconnect with ourselves, to be at peace and at ease with who we are and where we are going. All techniques in yoga aim to produce tranquillity; we will be covering postures, breath and relaxation with an added information page on meditation.

Through the processes and practices outlined for you, I hope you will take what you learn in your yoga practice and apply it to your daily living; then you will have received 'the gift of yoga'.

# POSTURES

Yoga postures should be both energising and relaxing, awakening and calming. The aim of postures is to bring the body, mind and spirit into harmony and equilibrium.

It is important to acknowledge the difference between yoga and an exercise program. Yoga is a mindful approach to the body, breath and mind. When we practise yoga, we must pay attention to ourselves and aim to be 'in' the postures rather than 'do' the postures.

To become present and mindful in your yoga practice, take mental notes: how is your body feeling in each posture? Is it aligned? Does it feel strong and energetic? How is your breath? Is it calm and smooth or short and sharp? Your mind – is it present or drifting off into what's happening next?

Yoga is about connection, receptivity, vulnerability and being present. Combining this awareness with the exercise component will ensure a more fulfilling practice.

*Introduction*

# BREATH

Breath is our life force; it nourishes all of our cells and our tissues and brings life into our being.

Human beings breathe about 15 times per minute. This respiration fuels the burning of oxygen and glucose, producing energy to power every muscle contraction, every heart beat, every mental process. Deep and slow breaths stimulate a calm, content state of mind and body.

The ancient yogis discovered the importance of deep breathing for added longevity and quality of life. They noticed that animals with slow breath rates, like elephants and tortoises, live longer than animals with faster breath rates, like birds, dogs and cats.

Yoga teaches us to deepen our breath, take control and re-establish the natural, relaxed rhythm of our body and mind.

# RELAXATION

The pace at which we live causes tremendous stress on our nervous system. We deal daily with such a bombardment of stimuli that our entire system ends up functioning at its very tethers.

When you take the time to understand and experience relaxation, you will discover that it is deeply rewarding and refreshing. The practice of relaxation seals the body's energy, helping to reset the nervous system and deliver increased energy into your entire being.

When we slow down, we create space for kindness, understanding and compassion to blossom. In essence, a relaxation practice will awaken your body, mind and heart to possibilities.

*Essential Yoga*

# ABOUT YOGA

*"In nature, action and reaction are continuous. Everything is connected to everything else; no one part is isolated. Everything is linked, and interdependent. Everywhere, everything is connected to everything else."*

— Swami Prajananpod

The word yoga means 'unity' and is derived from the Sanskrit word 'yuj' which means to join. The goal of yoga is to join, balance and harmonise the body, mind and emotions.

Through yoga practice, awareness develops of the inter-relation between the emotional, mental and physical connections and how a disturbance of any one of these affects the others.

Yoga allows you the precious time and space necessary for reflection. It is through the journey of discovery within that we find true happiness and joy. Once you have discovered your true organic self, you are free to approach life with trust, compassion, clarity and openness.

You can listen more clearly to the notes of the song in your heart; your body and mind can take on new forms of movement and grace as you follow your path. Once you are in touch with who you are, you can honour your own capacities, fears and feelings, along with those of others.

*About Yoga*

# BENEFITS OF YOGA

Yoga has a positive effect on the body's systems:

## MUSCLES AND LIGAMENTS

Increases strength and tone

Increases flexibility

Stimulates circulation

Helps correct poor posture and alignment

## SKELETAL SYSTEM

Strengthens and nourishes the spine

Increases joint mobility

Corrects alignment

Develops suppleness

## CIRCULATION

Massages heart and lungs

Strengthens pulmonary system

Increases blood flow

## NERVOUS SYSTEM

Increases neurotransmitters

Stabilises response of nervous system to stress

Reduces anxiety and tension

## GLANDS

Regulates hormonal production

Aids in cleansing the glands

Improves function of the glands

## IMMUNE SYSTEM

Removes toxins

Balances and strengthens the effectiveness of cells

Increases ability to fight infections

Stimulates glands and lymph nodes

## MIND

Increases clarity and concentration

Helps memory

Increases intuition

Increases self-awareness

## EMOTIONS

Brings a calmness

Generates an awareness of one's emotional being

Provides an inner strength and an ability to manage difficult situations with more confidence, clarity and grace.

*Essential Yoga*

# Principles of Postures

Every single posture, directly or indirectly, assists to quiet the mind. The primary purpose of the postures is to recondition your system, to enhance your physical, mental and spiritual well being.

Yoga should be practised to gain steady skeletal posture, balanced alignment, core strength and lightness of mind.

Many of the postures take their names from animals. Through their observation, ancient yogis noted that animals move in harmony with the environment and with themselves. If we can imitate animals, then perhaps we can move in harmony as well.

# Surrender/Letting go

The first main principle for effective yoga practice is the art of letting go: surrendering the internal and external body, learning how to soften and yield, not force or resist. This principle teaches us to allow the movement to come from our own natural strength and use our breath as a guide.

To explore the art of surrender, stand in your normal stance and observe your breath. Then gradually let your weight release down towards the ground, your muscles falling as if you have no bones. Feel your entire body sink down. Feel the release of harboured tension as you allow your body and mind to fully surrender.

The art of surrender is to find the balance between effort and ease without collapsing in the postures.

*About Yoga*

# GROUNDING

Grounding means connecting with the earth. Reconnecting ourselves with nature is essential for finding our foundations. When we isolate ourselves in cars and high rise buildings, we estrange ourselves from the Earth, the stars and the heavens. Yoga can help us rediscover that we are an important part of the universe.

Grounding is the second principle to effective posture work. You must be aware of your foundations in all of your postures, feel which parts of your body are on the ground. Maintain this awareness of your foundations throughout all of your posture work.

To explore the grounding principle, come into Mountain posture and observe which parts of your body are on the ground. Press into these foundations until you feel the Earth pressing back. Observe the uplift of all other parts of your body as they rise with the Earth's energy.

# ALIGNMENT

Alignment creates a harmonious flow of energy and produces a clear pathway through the body with space between the joints and muscles. Consider the bones as they carry the muscles. Improving alignment creates a synergy of bones and muscles working together. Muscles become more supple and strong, and allow the energy to flow more effectively.

To find good alignment, stand in Mountain posture. Notice the direction of your feet: place them facing forward from the knees, your weight spread evenly. Place your knees above your ankles, hips above knees, torso rising upwards, shoulders, neck and head lifting. Take note: are your bones and muscles working effectively together? Can you feel the symmetry of your body?

Alignment comes from surrender and grounding and leads into ease of breath.

*Essential Yoga*

# BREATH

Most of the time, we are not aware of our breath. The practice of yoga, however, encourages us to take notice, encouraging deep and efficient breathing.

As we get older, we tend to breathe more into the chest rather than the abdomen. This may occur through stress, injury, postural problems or emotional distress. It is vital for our overall wellbeing to re-train our bodies in deep, full abdominal breathing.

Practising yoga breathing will stretch and tone the muscles of the chest, diaphragm and abdomen, and improve the mobility and elasticity of the lungs. This in turn purifies the bloodstream, cleans the sinuses, soothes and tones the nervous system and calms and concentrates the mind.

To explore a deep breath practice, lie flat on your back; place your hands on your belly and inhale. Draw the breath to the deepest part of your lungs and feel your belly rise. Notice now how your ribcage expands and your chest lifts when you fill your lungs into their depths. When you breathe out, exhale in a smooth continuous movement, observing the belly lowering under your hands.

Full natural breathing occurs when we balance effort and ease in our postures. When we surrender, ground and align, we can discover freedom in postures and breathing.

# Preparing to Practise

*When the mind fluctuations have dwindled, consciousness becomes like a transparent jewel, residing in the pure essence of itself.*

— Patañjali

## Create your Space

Creating a space for your home yoga practice can be a challenge: there are distractions and interruptions, and some days you just won't feel like practising. It's a good idea to sit down and look at your schedule and see where you can fit yoga into your weekly program. Some days you may only have twenty minutes, other days you may have more time.

If you don't live alone, let others know that you are going to spend some time practising yoga so that you are not interrupted. Ideally, switch your phone off for this short period of time.

Practise anywhere in the house where you feel comfortable and relaxed. It can be a small corner of the living room, your bedroom or a separate room that is set up for your yoga practice, but ensure wherever you choose has a nice, even floor. You can also light a few candles or burn some incense to add to the atmosphere.

## Prepare your Body and Mind

Each day before you practise, ask yourself, how am I feeling today? Do I feel like working strongly or softly, fast or slow? What is the state of my breath – is it calm or choppy, deep or shallow?

It is important to pay attention to how you feel on a daily basis. Just because you worked hard and moved through some strong postures yesterday does not mean that you will do the same today.

Each day, even from morning until evening, we have different needs. Listen to your body; focus on what each new day brings. Yoga is about the subtle soft changes and building awareness of 'self'.

Try to wait at least 3 hours after a main meal, and one hour after a light snack before practising. Empty the bladder and the bowels too, if possible.

# Yoga Tools

- Yoga mat – to prevent your hands, feet or elbows from slipping on the floor and to give you greater support in your posture work.
- A blanket – to keep warm during relaxation. As your body relaxes, your blood pressure drops and your body cools. It is important to keep yourself warm in order to enter a deeper relaxation.
- Eye pillow – to assist in relaxation. Eye pillows rest on the pressure points around your eyes and shut out light.
- Comfortable clothing – to ensure comfort and ease of movement.
- Chimes – to provide soothing sounds that bring a sense of peace and balance to the environment.

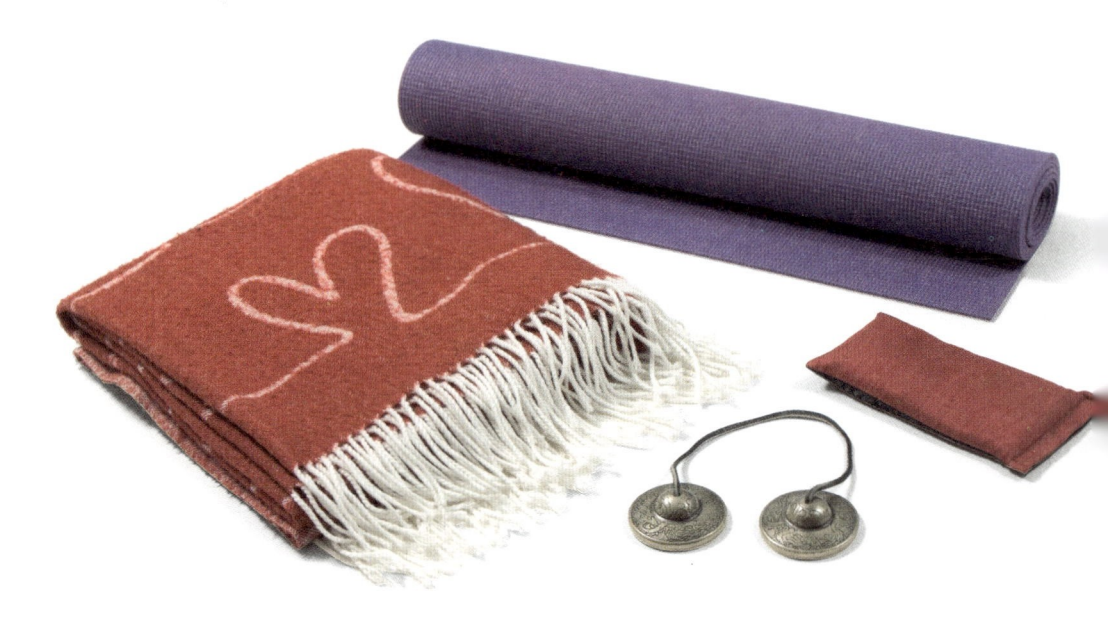

# Workouts

A full yoga workout is ideal, but there will be some times when your body will require something specific. I've created four specialised workouts to target certain moods and needs.

Although a relaxation section is not included in these modified workouts, I recommend that you do a few minutes of relaxation at the end of each program.

## Energising

An energising program will give you an energy boost and awaken your body and mind. Benefits include an increase in the effectiveness of your cardiovascular system, an increase in blood flow to your muscles, organs, and glands, and a renewed energy through your entire being.

For an energising workout, combine the Warm Up, Sun Salutations, Standing Postures and Backward Bends.

## Strengthening

Strengthening workouts increase your strength and energy. By developing awareness of grounding and foundation principles, increasing strength, and improving alignment, strengthening programs also improve posture and energy flow.

For a strengthening workout, combine the Warm Up, Standing Postures, Balances and Backward Bends.

## Flexibility

Flexibility programs will increase flexibility and range of motion in your muscles and joints. Moving through a flexibility program will increase movement through your joints, lengthen shortened muscles, release tension in blocked areas of your body, and untangle the knots that affect daily energy levels.

For a flexibility workout, combine the Warm Up, Sun Salutations, Backward Bends, Forward Bends and Spinal Twists.

## Relaxation

A relaxation program quiets the body and mind, and teaches you how to slow down and create space for awareness. A regular relaxation program will reset your nervous system and bring vitality and freshness into your entire being.

For a relaxation workout, combine the Warm Up, Balances, Forward Bends, Spinal Twists and Relaxation.

# Warm Up

This is the place
where the journey begins.
Half rooted into the earth,
half floating in the endless sky.
What would it be like
to be the mountain?

— Leza Lowitz

*Essential Yoga*

Warm ups prepare the body for yoga sequencing. A good warm up enhances blood flow to the muscles, joints, tendons and ligaments. Warm ups also introduce the principles of yoga and teach the nervous system to respond.

# MOUNTAIN POSTURE
## Tadasana

1. Line your feet up with your thigh bones, knees above ankles, hips and torso aligned. Place your feet firmly into the ground, hips lifted, sternum lifted, shoulders and arms relaxed, top of head rising upwards to the sky.

2. Spread your toes; feel the balls of your feet and your heels connecting to the ground. Press down powerfully through your feet until you feel the earth pushing back. Let this push expand up through your shin bones, front thighs and torso. Feel how your body lengthens and lifts, growing into the space above your head.

3. Imagine a string gently lifting the crown of your head. While keeping your body strong, soften your ears, shoulders and jaw. Soften internally but keep your physical shell strong.

4. Focus on full deep breaths: feel the rising of your abdomen as you draw the breath into the depths of the lungs and feel the air fully release, allowing a greater intake on the next breath.

*Warm Up*

# Arm & Shoulder Warming

**1** Move your arms forward and upwards with your breath, extending fully through your torso and into your finger tips as you lift your body upwards.

**2** Lengthen your arms away from your body as you breathe out. Imagine your arms moving through water and feel the resistance.

**3** Allow your arms to soften beside your body before you inhale and repeat twice more.

# Butterfly Hands

**1** With hands interlocked, breathe in and watch your hands as they lift past your eyes and then upwards, lengthening your entire front torso.

**2** Allow your eyes to follow the path of your hands as you breathe out, lowering your arms back down to your body.

**3** Allow your arms to soften, hands still interlocked, before you repeat twice more.

*Essential Yoga*

# SPINAL WARMING

1. Place your hands behind your head, tilting your head gently downwards.

2. On the next breath in, lift upwards with your head, draw your elbows back and open your chest as you tilt your pelvis back.

3. On the breath out, lower your head, draw your elbows together and tilt your pelvis forward. Move fully from the top of your spine to the bottom of your spine. Repeat twice more.

*Warm Up*

# Head Tilts/Neck Stretch

**1** Allow your head to drop to one side.

**2** Take your hand and place it on the opposite shoulder.

**3** Gently press down on your shoulder, allow the muscles of your neck to lengthen as your head tilts closer to your other shoulder.

**4** Repeat on the other side.

*Essential Yoga*

# LATERAL STRETCH

**1** Stretch one hand straight up to the sky, the other hand down towards the Earth. Feel the space created in your chest and shoulders.

**2** Begin to tilt and lengthen the side of your body. Feel the entire side of your torso lengthening, your ribcage expanding, your breath flowing naturally.

**3** Come back to centre and then repeat to the other side.

# STANDING SPINAL TWIST
*Parivritti Tadasana*

**1** Breathe in and reach one hand over to the opposite shoulder and the other hand behind you to the opposite hip. Looking over your back shoulder, allow your breath to help you rotate and twist.

**2** Return to the centre and repeat to other side.

*Warm Up*

# ELEPHANT

**1** Standing in Mountain posture, allow your body to drift downwards, folding from your hips — head, shoulders and arms relaxed.

**2** Walk your legs out wider than your hips. Take one hand into the other hand, holding gently. Imagine your arms are the trunk of an elephant and, very slowly, move from hip to hip, releasing tension from your body as you breathe evenly.

**3** Release your arms as your return to centre. Walk your legs back into alignment with your hips and then, pressing into your feet, move your body upwards one vertebra at a time until your head is the last to lift.

*Essential Yoga*

# STANDING FORWARD BEND
## Uttanasana

**1** Arrange your feet hip-width apart in Mountain posture. Begin to fold from your hips and allow your upper body to hang over your lower body.

**2** Place your hands behind your legs, hands interlocked. Press into your feet and draw the energy up your legs, (knees can be bent slightly).

**3** With each breath in, lift and lengthen your front torso slightly. With each breath out, lengthen more from your hamstrings, lifting your pelvis upwards, allowing your upper body to fold over more thoroughly.

*Warm Up*

# SPINAL ROLLS

**1** Start from a Standing Forward Bend, feet pressing into the ground. Moving slowly and consciously, roll up one vertebra at a time until you are standing in an upright Mountain posture again.

**2** From Mountain posture, begin to lower your head, shoulders and neck, releasing back down one vertebra at a time.

**3** Feel the surrender as you roll down and engage your connection with the Earth, working strongly through your entire body as you lift up.

**4** Repeat twice more.

*Essential Yoga*

# STANDING CAT
## Marichyasana

**1** Standing in Mountain posture, fold forward and place your hands above your knees.

**2** Breathe in, arch your back and look at your belly, tilt your hips in. Imagine a scared cat.

**3** Breathe out, arching your back in the opposite direction by tilting your head up and your hips away. Imagine forming a crescent moon shape with your back, first in one direction and then in the other.

**4** Repeat twice more.

# STANDING CHEST OPENER

**1** Standing in Mountain posture, place your hands on your hips, draw your elbows back and open wide through your chest and shoulders.

# Sun Salutations

Today a new sun rises for me; everything lives, everything is animated, everything seems to speak to me of my passion, everything invites me to cherish it.

— Ninon de Lenclos

## Essential Yoga

The flow of movement through the Sun Salutations connects balancing, forward bending, backward bending and centring postures. By linking poses together through movement and breath, this practice uses the whole body and improves suppleness.

Sun Salutations energise, increase the effectiveness of the cardiovascular system and create balance and harmony between the body, breath and mind.

# SUN SALUTATIONS SEQUENCE
## Surya Namaskar

1. Stand with your feet positioned in line with your thigh bones, your toes spread on the floor, your heels grounded. Keep your legs strong and lifting upwards, your torso rising upwards, top of your head lifting to the sky. Place your hands with palms together in front of your chest near your heart.

2. Breathe in and lift your arms upwards above your head.

## Sun Salutations

**3** Breathe out and fold forward from your hips into a Standing Forward Bend.

**4** Breathe in as you bend your knees and lengthen your spine, top of your head moving forward, tail moving behind you.

**5** Breathe out, step back into a lunge and take a deep breath in while pushing into your legs, deepening your hips.

# Essential Yoga

**6** Breathe out and step your opposite leg back into Downward Facing Dog. Press onto your hands, weight on index finger and thumb, lift your hips high and press your feet firmly into the floor.

**7** Breathe in, move from your toes, lengthening your body forward, keeping your back and abdomen strong, and hold yourself like a plank.

**8** Breathe out, lower to low plank or onto knees.

## Sun Salutations

**9** Breathe in and move into Upward Facing Dog by coming onto your belly, shoulders and chest broad, feet and legs holding your weight and lifting you upwards.

**10** Breathe out. From Upwards Facing Dog, curl your toes under and lift your hips back into Downwards Facing Dog. Press into your hands and feet, and lift your hips high.

**11** Breathe in again and, as you breathe out, step your leading foot (the one that first stepped back in step 5) forward into lunge position. Breathe in and press into your legs.

31

# Essential Yoga

**12** Breathe out and step your back leg forward in line with your front leg.

**13** Stand into Standing Forward Bend. Breathe in and lift upwards with your torso and arms.

**14** Breathe out and allow your arms to come beside your body, back to Mountain posture.

Begin this sequence again on the other side.

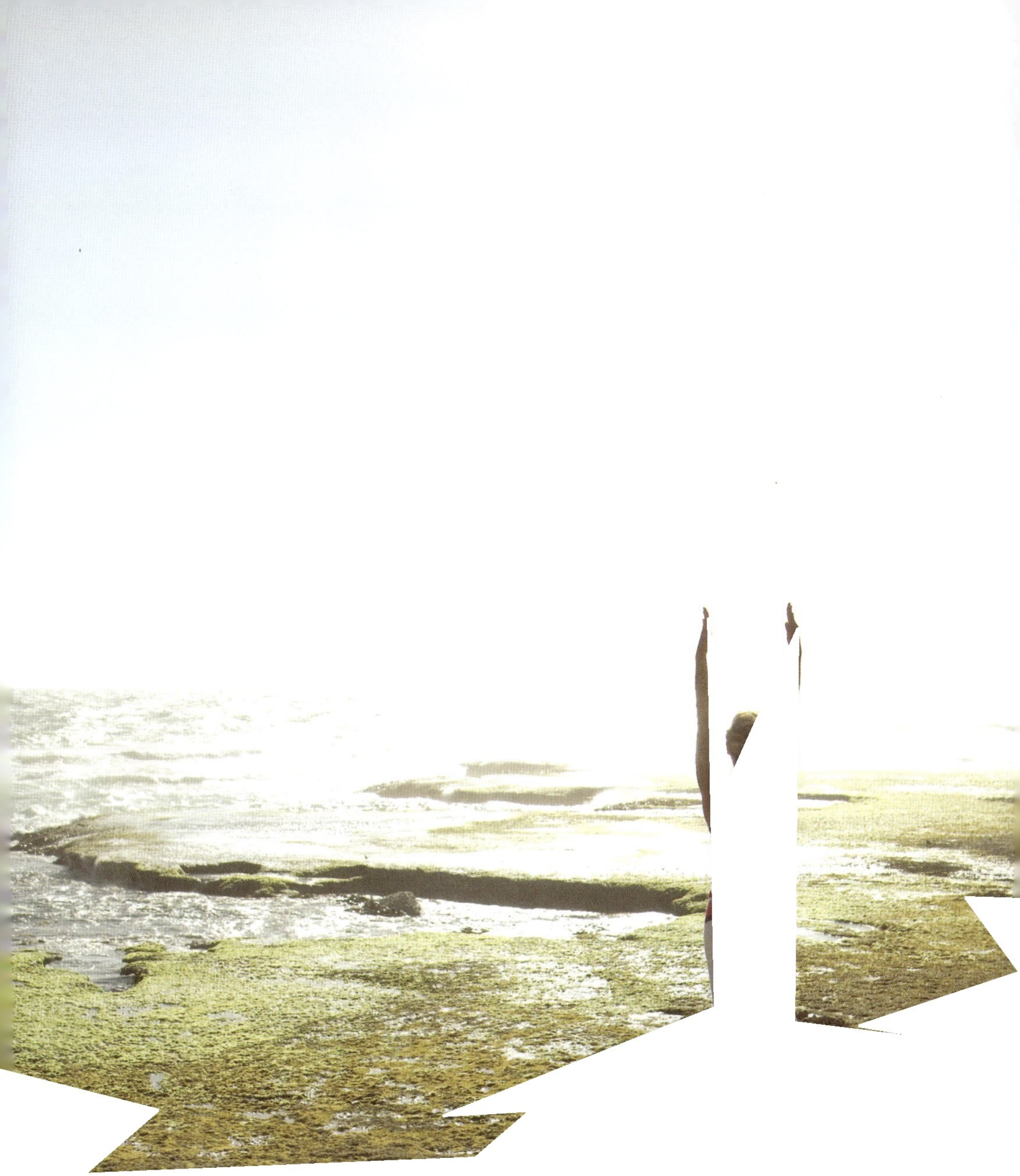

# Standing postures

Here there is nothing to fight
Except wilfulness.
Some lean too far
Into the past.
Others stretch way out
Into the future.
The true warrior
Stays in the moment,
Burning deeper
Into whatever comes,
Or sometimes with
Even more difficulty,
What doesn't.

— Leza Lowitz

## Standing postures

Standing postures are vigorous postures: they awaken your connection with the Earth. The soles of your feet draw the breath up your body from the ground below. In standing postures, your entire being is awakened and brought into the present.

It is important to keep in mind the surrendering, grounding and alignment principles in these postures. Relax your body, feel your connections, and make minor adjustments to your alignment to ensure a flow of energy.

The following group of standing postures stimulates the nervous system, aids in improving the digestive system, strengthens the legs and pelvic area, and tones the reproductive organs.

# WARRIOR 2
## Virabvadvasana

1. Stand in Mountain posture, then move your feet wider than your hips. Turn your front foot to a 90 degree angle in the direction you are going to begin, your back foot to a 30 degree angle in the same direction. Let go of any tension in your body.

2. Firm your thighs and ensure your knees are aligned above your ankles. Bend your front knee, shin and ankle and push into your back leg. Feel the strength in your legs.

3. Stretch your arms out wide, checking to be sure they are at the same level. Reaching long through your arms and deep in your legs, focus on your long middle finger. Allow your breath to flow, adjust the posture and feel the energy flow through your body from the ground.

*Essential Yoga*

# EXTENDED WARRIOR
### Parsvakonasana

**1** From Warrior 2 posture, breathe in and lower your elbow to your knee, reaching your other arm upwards to the ceiling or across the body, lengthening from your hips to your finger tips.

**2** Turn your belly, chest and head upwards, keeping your shoulder released away from your ear.

# DANCING WARRIOR
### Viparita Virribradvasana

**1** From Extended Warrior posture, move your upper torso upwards, keeping your legs deep and strong. Lower your back hand down your back leg, raise your top hand above your head. Imagine a warrior dancing.

**2** Repeat this sequence of Warrior 2, Extended Warrior and Dancing Warrior to the other side.

*Standing postures*

# TRIANGLE
*Trikonasana*

1. Take a wide stance with your legs. Move your front foot to a 90 degree angle in the direction you are going to begin, your back foot to a 30 degree angle in the same direction. Relax and let your weight fall.

2. As you press into your feet and feel the energy rising up through your body, begin to spread your arms out long, palms forward, staying long in your waist, moving from your hips, keeping your legs long and strong.

3. Fold to the side in the direction of your front foot. Let your hand rest where it falls, whether that is on your shin or lower or higher. Look up to your top hand, keeping your head in a neutral position, ear away from shoulder.

4. Imagine that you are a starfish, your limbs spreading out from the centre of your body. Feel your breath flowing and notice your ribs opening with each breath. Continue to adjust the posture and feel how a small adaptation can help you to really enjoy the posture and feel the energy flowing.

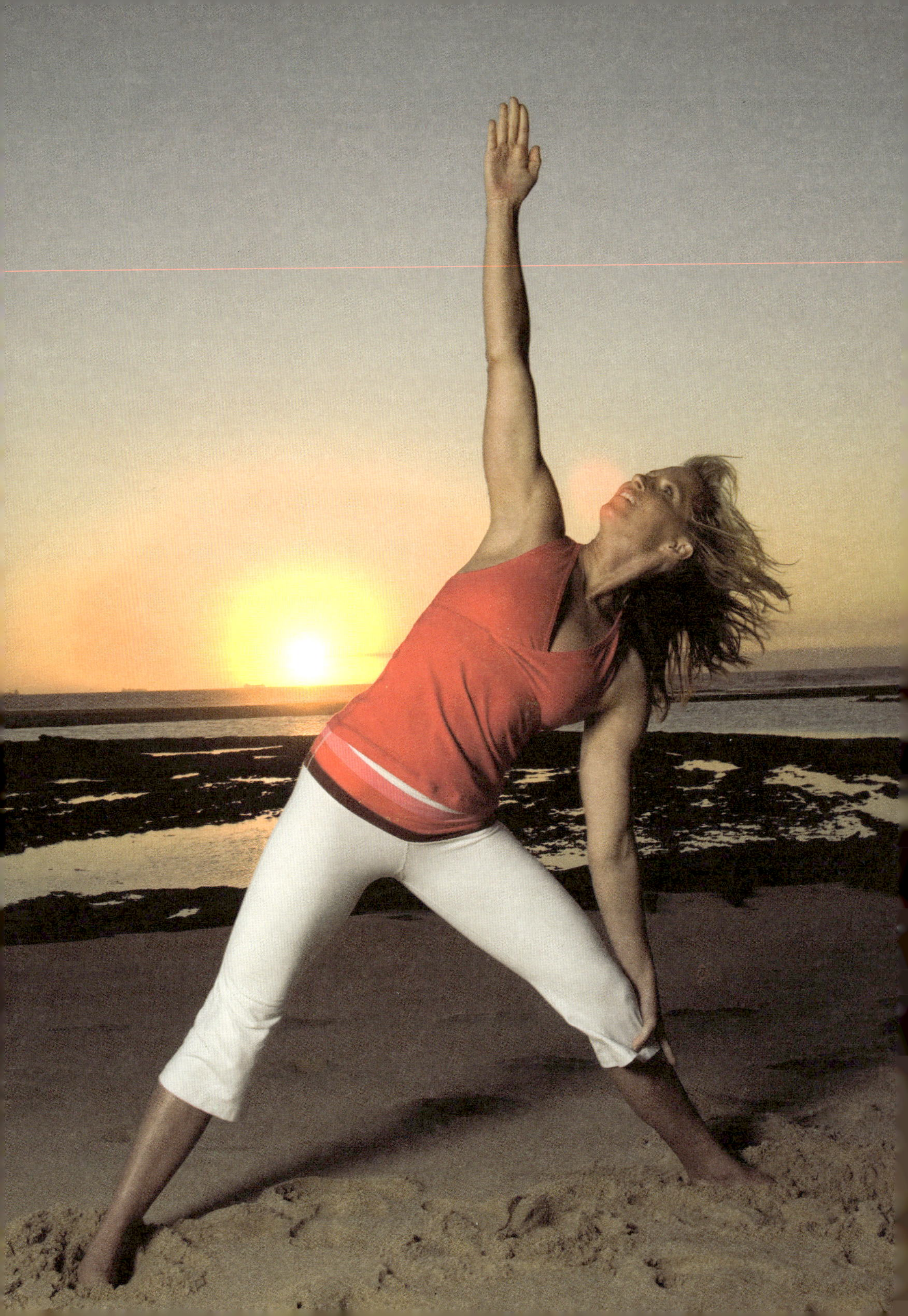

# Balances

O to be self-balanced for contingencies,
To confront night, storms, hunger, ridicule,
accidents, rebuffs as the trees and
the animals do.

- Walt Whitman

*Essential Yoga*

Balances help promote connection, receptivity and being present. Balances also allow us to challenge ourselves to develop courage, strength and willpower.

The following group of postures helps balance the nervous system, develop control of the body and mental connection and increase strength.

# Toe/Heel Combo

1. Moving forward onto your toes, rotate your hands inwards away from your body. Slowly lower back to neutral as you breathe out, softening your hands beside your body.

2. Move onto your heels, rotating your hands outwards away from your body. Slowly lower to neutral as you breathe out, softening your hands beside your body.

3. Continue moving, first onto your toes and then onto your heels with the breath. Repeat these movements 3 times.

# Tree
## Vrksasana

1. Standing in Mountain posture, draw one heel up to your inner thigh and place your palms together in the centre of your chest.

2. Press into your grounding leg and rise up through the centre of your body, growing tall from the Earth to the sky as a tree does in nature.

3. Breathe calmly and smoothly as you lengthen your arms upwards towards the sky. Movement is ok, but try to find a focus point to help you balance.

4. Move your hands back into the centre of your chest and lower your leg down.

Balances

# DANCER
## Natarajasana

1. Moving from Mountain posture, take one leg behind you and wrap your hand around your ankle or foot. Stay relaxed, pressing into the ground.

2. With your opposite hand, begin to lift your arm away from your body. As you move your front arm away from your body, your back leg moves further away behind you.

3. Imagine a beautiful dancer, gliding out and opening up, lifting away. Hips maintain a rolling position, spine long and arms and legs moving away from your torso.

# EAGLE
## Garudasana

1. Move from Mountain posture, bend your knees, slightly lowering your hips. Lift one leg off the ground and wrap that leg around your grounded leg.

2. Stretch your arms forward, one arm bending and coming close to your chest and your opposite arm wrapping around the outside of the arm close to your chest and coming up on the inside of your wrist, palms facing each other.

3. Lower down slightly by bending your legs and lift slightly from your arms in an upward and outward direction. Imagine soaring like an eagle in the sky.

4. Release and repeat this sequence of Tree, Dancer and Eagle to the other side.

*Essential Yoga*

# TRANSITIONAL SEQUENCE

This series of poses will allow you to move easily from the standing postures to the floor. The transitional sequence is very similar to the first few steps of the Sun Salutations.

1. Start in Mountain posture, ankles, knees, and hips aligned, hands and arms relaxed by your sides.

2. Breathe in and lift your arms above your head.

3. Breathe out and fold forward from your hips into a Standing Forward Bend.

4. Breathe in as you bend your knees and lengthen your spine, top of your head moving forward, tail moving behind you.

# Balances

**5** Breathe out, step back into a lunge and take a deep breath in while pushing into your legs, deepening your hips.

**6** Breathe out and step your opposite leg back into Downward Facing Dog. Press onto your hands, weight on index finger and thumb, lift your hips high and press your feet firmly into the floor.

**7** Breathe in, move from your toes, lengthening your body forward, keeping your back and abdomen strong, and hold yourself like a plank.

**8** Breathe out, lower to your belly on the floor.

# Backward bends

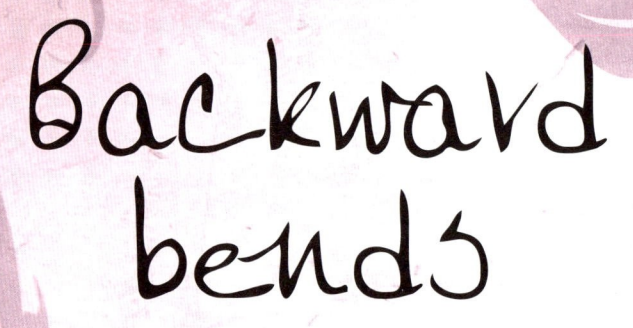

Open the heart
and the heart opens you-
salt of the creator,
eye of the beholder
stretch your arms overhead
receive
the rainfall of pure clarity...
Open the heart
and the heart opens you.

— Leza Lowitz

## Backward bends

**B**ackward bends open the heart chakra, the emotional centre of your being where you experience joy and grief. This requires the willingness to connect to your emotional centre and to be open to feeling both intense joy and happiness, and grief and despair.

Most of us have a habitual pattern of bending slightly forward, rounding the shoulders into the chest. Therefore it is important to add backward bends into your program to rebalance neck, shoulders, pelvis and spine.

These vigorous backward bends require concentration, and strengthen the muscles and nerves of the back, and tone the internals organs.

# LOCUST
## Salabasana

1. Lie flat on your belly with your arms along the side of your torso, forehead resting on the floor and legs long behind you, back muscles broadening.

2. Breathe out and lift your head, upper torso, arms and legs away from the floor. Firm your buttocks and reach strongly through your legs.

3. Stretch back evenly through your arms and gaze forward to keep the spine long. Length is more important than height for this posture; be sure to maintain a flowing, even breath.

4. Slowly lower and allow your head to rest to one side and then repeat once more.

*Essential Yoga*

# Half Bow
## Ardha Danurasana

**1** Lie flat on your belly with your legs and feet together and long. Bend one knee, bringing your foot near your buttocks.

**2** Reach back with your hand to your foot, use your opposite hand to push your upper body upwards and begin to lengthen and lift your foot away from your body. Allow your spine to move evenly and listen to your breath.

**3** Begin to lengthen and lift the foot away from your body. Feel your spine and your chest move evenly away from your body.

**4** Release and lie flat on your belly.

# Bow
## Danurasana

**1** Lie flat on your belly with your hands alongside your torso. Breathe out and bend your knees, bringing your heels as close as you can to your buttocks.

**2** Reach back with your hands and take hold of your ankles. Make sure your knees stay close together and lined up with your hips.

**3** Breathe in and lift your heels away from your buttocks. At the same time, lift your upper torso away from the floor. Maintain a constant, even movement of the spine throughout the posture, your breath remaining even and smooth.

**4** Release and lie flat on your belly.

46

Backward bends

# Extended Puppy
Uttana Shishosana

1. Move up to all fours. Check that your shoulders are above your wrists and hips above your knees. Curl your toes under.

2. As you breathe out, press your hands into the ground and move your hips back towards your heels.

3. Drop your forehead towards the floor and allow your neck to relax, arms extended forward and front body lengthening.

4. Breathe into your back and feel your spine lengthen in both directions.

# Upwards Dog
Urdhva Mukha Svanasana

1. Moving from Extended Puppy pose, as you inhale, flatten your feet and move your hips forward by pressing into the ground with your hands.

2. Press off your legs as you support your upper torso, lifting upwards. Maintain an open chest by lowering your shoulders back and away from your ears.

3. As you breathe out, move back to Extended Puppy pose and as you breathe in move into Upwards Dog.

4. Repeat these movements 3 times.

# HALF BRIDGE
## Setubandasana

1. Lie flat on your back and bend your knees, heels as close as possible to your buttocks. Your arms should lie beside your body with palms facing downwards. Surrender the weight of your body to the ground.

2. Breathe out and press your feet and arms into the floor. Begin to lift your buttocks until your thighs are parallel to the floor. Make sure your knees remain above your heels and your tailbone lengthens towards the back of your knees.

3. Press onto your arms, back of shoulders and feet, noticing as you consciously press onto your foundations how the rest of your body can rise up higher. Continue to aim your chest and belly higher as you hold this posture.

4. Keep your awareness on pressing your foundations into the ground and enable the rest of your body to rise up. Breath should be even and steady.

## Backward bends
# DYNAMIC HALF BRIDGE
## Dynamic Setu Bandasana

1. Lie flat on your back and bend your knees, heels as close as possible to your buttocks. Arms lie along side your body.

2. Breathe in and press your feet and arms to the floor. Begin to lift your buttocks and, at the same time, lift your arms, raising them upwards and behind you as you lift your hips.

3. Breathe out, lowering your arms and hips slowly back to the ground. You want to move the hips and arms together, both rising and lowering at the same time.

4. Repeat 3 times.

*Essential Yoga*

# Knee-Hug and Rock

**1** Hug your knees.

**2** When you can feel your hipbones in contact with the floor, rock side to side.

# Happy Baby
## Ananda Balasana

**1** Lie on your back and hug your knees towards your chest. Lift your heels upwards, place your hands on top of your feet and widen your legs.

**2** Move your feet and legs around and enjoy the feeling of your back being supported and hips being released.

# Forward bends

*When the posture of yoga is steady and easy, resting like a cosmic serpent on the waters of infinity, then one is unconstrained by opposing dualities.*

— Patañjali

*Essential Yoga*

Forward bends assist in stretching the hamstring muscles, increasing the flexibility in the hip joints, massaging the abdominal organs and improving the digestive system.

Forward bends have a quieting effect, rejuvenating the nervous system and calming the emotions. Forward bends allow time to focus on what is happening within the body and mind.

# FORWARD BEND SEQUENCE
## Sukhasana

1. Sit upright, legs crossed in front of you. Feet are flexed.

2. Press into your buttocks and reach forward with your belly, chest and fingertips, keeping your shoulder blades down and your spine long. Allow your breath to flow evenly and deeply as your body lowers.

3. Moving from a cross leg sit posture, turn your belly to the side so your torso is over one thigh and fold forward, your knee positioned in the middle of your arms. Continue moving your belly, chest and finger tips in a forward direction feeling the lengthening of your spine with each breath.

# Forward bends

4. Come back into centre, place one hand near your hip for support and raise your other hand over your head, stretching the side of your body. Focus your eyes on your top hand and maintain the space between your shoulder and ear.

5. Come back into centre and place the lifted arm on your opposite knee. Turn your belly, chest and shoulders in that direction. Breathe in and lift up through your shoulders, neck and head.

6. Breathe out and allow your body to rotate around your spine, looking at your back shoulder.

7. Come back into centre. Repeat this sequence to the other side.

# Spinal Twists

We are all on a spiral path,
Growth does not occur in straight lines.
There will be challenges along the way,
There will be shadows.
But they will be balanced with whispers of joy
And baskets of happiness.

## Spinal Twists

Spinal twist postures cleanse emotionally and physically, by allowing a release, and a softening through the body and mind. As you meet limitations in twists, you can learn the art of not forcing to overcome but sit with the resistance and let go.

Spinal twists are nourishing to the spine: they increase blood flow and nerve supply to the spinal column, release and cleanse toxins from the body and aid in massaging the digestive system.

# Seated Spinal Twist
## Half Ardha Matsyendrasana

1. Sitting on the floor, extend one leg out in front of you. Bend your opposite knee and place it over your long leg.

2. Take your opposite arm to your bent knee and hug the crook of your elbow around your knee. Place your opposite hand behind you near your hip.

3. Breathe in, pressing into your buttocks and lengthening your spine upwards.

4. Breathe out, rotate and twist around the spinal column, softening as you exhale. Don't force the stretch but allow it to deepen.

5. Release back to centre and swap sides.

*Essential Yoga*

# Rolling Spinal Twist
## Dynamic Jathara Parivritti

**1** Roll down from sitting, lie on your side with your knees stacked on top of each other, arms and hands also stacked.

**2** Take your top hand and gently follow the line of the bottom arm and across your chest, placing that hand on the opposite side of your body.

**3** Begin to roll your knees to the other side, placing your hands and knees on top of each other again.

**4** Continue rolling side to side; enjoy the feeling of your body surrendering.

56

## Spinal Twists

# LYING SPINAL TWIST
## Jathara Parivritti

**1** Lie flat on your back, bend one knee and keep your other leg long on the ground. Place the bent leg on the thigh of your long leg and then slowly roll to your long leg side.

**2** Place your top hand on the bent knee and assist in lowering that knee towards the ground. Your other hand should be relaxed beside you, eyes looking towards your opposite shoulder.

**3** Lengthen and spread your body on the ground, soften the muscles and allow the body to rotate. Surrender your mind to the breath.

# Relaxation & Meditation

Slow and deep
into the heart of the day.
With each inhalation
comes an exhalation
twice as long.
Slow and deep
filling the lungs
with infinite space,
the sun rises and sets
in each single breath.

— Leza Lowitz

*Relaxation & Meditation*

# MEDITATION

*Do you have the patience to wait till your mud settles and the water is clear? Can you remain unmoving till the right action arises by itself?*

— *Lao Tzu*

Meditation is the practice of becoming detached from and a witness to the mind. A quiet mind protects us against the stresses of everyday life. Meditation assists us in finding health and happiness by taking us back to our true nature, back to ourselves.

Newcomers to meditation may find it difficult at first to sit and turn their attention inward. Our attention normally goes outward in order to cope with the challenges of our environment. Looking within can reveal a lot of chatter. Meditation sets out to reduce that internal noise and take you to a place of peace, to open spaces between thoughts, to somewhere where the waters have smoothed out.

Have you observed that when your mind is disturbed, your body fidgets more? Or, whenever your body is fidgeting, your mind cannot be still? You are not divided in two. What affects the body also affects the mind, and vice versa. That is why it is so important that we work together on the body and mind in yoga.

# Aids to Meditation or Relaxation

Many imaginative techniques can be used to aid in meditation and relaxation; here are three:

Imagine that you are lying on a beach, listening to the soothing sounds of the sea. Feel the soft caress of the gentle breeze and the warmth of the sunshine on your body. Feel the ebb and flow of the sea flowing through your body and float away.

Visualise a current of water gently flowing over your body, cleansing your mind and body of all tensions and impurities. Imagine the cleansing that occurs as the refreshing water flows over your neck, across your shoulders, arms, chest and then continues to flow down the length of your spine, over your abdomen and torso, across the buttocks, thighs, legs and feet. As the water flows, your body and mind become more flexible and fluid. Life is movement; the more fluid you are, the more alive you feel.

Focus on your breath: follow it from the entrance of your nostrils, down the back of your throat and into your lungs. Draw the breath into the deepest part of your lungs, completely filling them with renewed oxygen. Feel the abdomen rise as the lungs fill, notice how the abdomen and chest can expand and lift. Now follow the path of breath back out of your body. Notice how the abdomen lowers, the ribcage comes back together and the chest settles as the breath flows back out of your body, emptying the lungs completely. Let go.

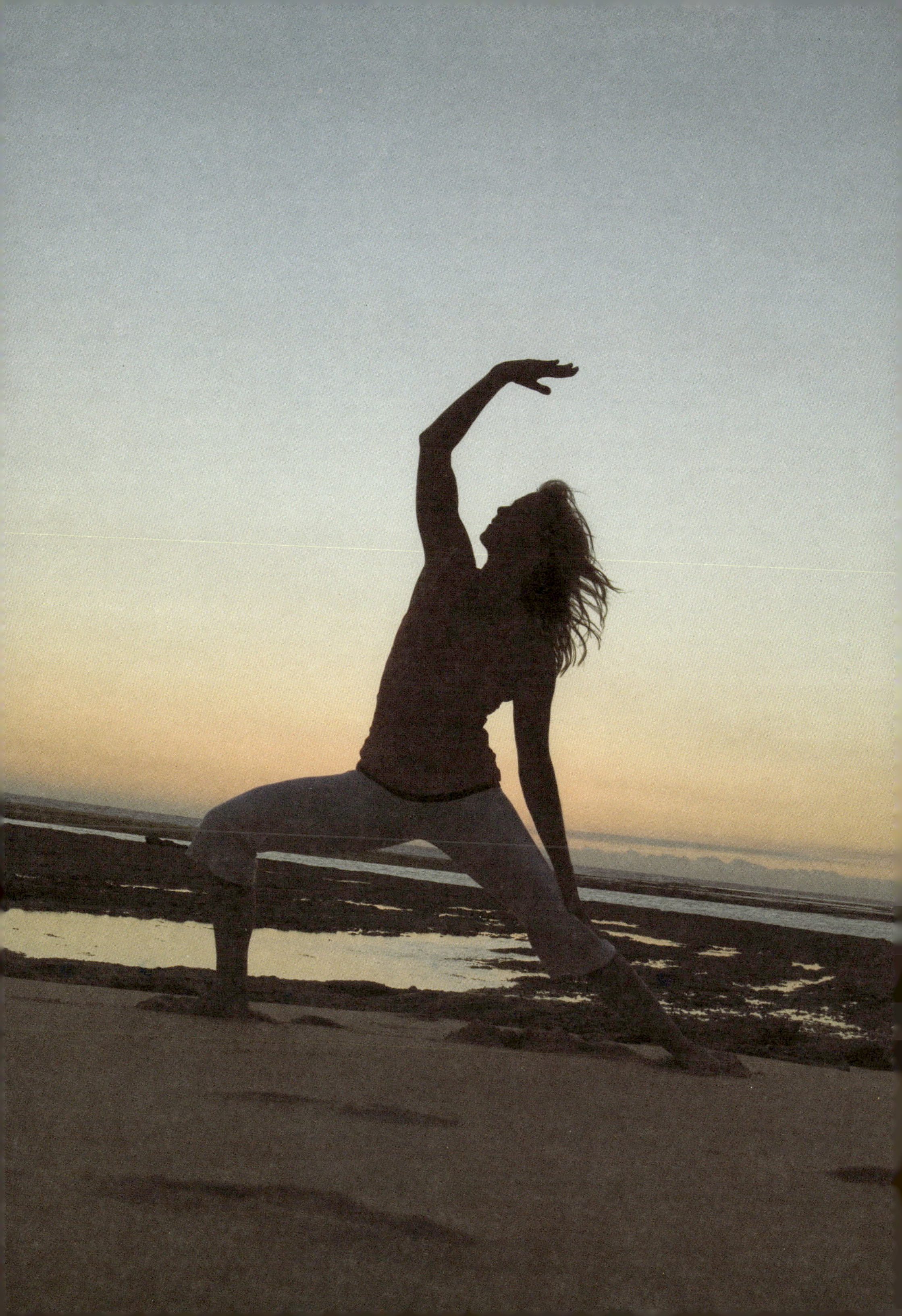

*Essential Yoga*

# CONCLUSION

The aim of this book was to introduce the principles of yoga and self discovery.

By learning some of the key components of postures, breathing and relaxation, you now have tools that can be used anytime to enhance your physical and emotional wellbeing.

Posture work will assist you in increasing your strength and your flexibility, aid you in awakening yourself when you need an increase in energy, and help you find peace when you need to.

Understanding and using your breath will nourish you from the inside out, and fill you with energy and vitality.

Finally, relaxation techniques will help bring your body, mind and emotions back into equilibrium.

Remember, these skills are like any other – they require time and practice. The beauty is that practice is not only rejuvenating, but also rewarding.

*Essential Yoga* will allow you to stay grounded and in your centre no matter what storms are brewing around you, to understand that there is peace and happiness within, and that, at any moment, at any point in the day, you can come back into yourself, back to 'home'.

# GLOSSARY

CHAKRA: From the Sanskrit, meaning circle or wheel. Chakras are commonly described as the energy centres of the body.

GLANDULAR SYSTEM (Glands): The system of the body that controls hormone production and release.

IMMUNE SYSTEM: The system of the body that protects against disease by identifying and killing viruses, pathogens and tumours.

LIGAMENTS: Fibrous tissue that connects bones to other bones.

LYMPH NODES: Part of the lymphatic system, lymph nodes work as filters and traps for foreign particles and contain white blood cells.

MUSCLES: A tissue of the body whose function is to produce force and cause motion, either locomotion or movement within the internal organs.

NERVOUS SYSTEM: A highly specialised network of tissue that conduct stimuli via electrochemical signals. At its very base, the nervous system controls all our reactions, voluntary and involuntary to what's happening around us.

NEUROTRANSMITTERS: The chemicals that are used to relay messages in the body.

PULMONARY SYSTEM: The system of the body that controls breathing and the exchange of oxygen.

SKELETAL SYSTEM: The system of the body that provides physical support to the body.

VERTEBRA: The individual bones that make up the spinal column.

YOGI: one who practises various forms of the path of yoga. This designation is reserved for advanced or daily practitioners.

*Essential Yoga*

# ABOUT THE AUTHOR

Gena Kenny has worked in the health and fitness industry as a lecturer and instructor since 1990. She was also a full time firefighter with the Melbourne Fire Brigade in Australia for 13 years. Passionate about the balance of hatha style yoga, she has taught to diverse groups such as elite athletes, senior citizens, people suffering with multiple sclerosis and those seeking improved flexibility and strength.

First introduced to yoga while recovering from an injury, Gena sees yoga as a gift and has gained much more through her yoga than just physical recovery. She credits yoga with helping her discover the path to self awareness and enlightenment of her life's purpose. Connecting the spirit of yoga with the essence of nature, Gena hopes to share the treasures of personal development and growth with others.

As a fitness enthusiast, Gena has been instrumental in the formation of outrigger canoeing as a sport in Victoria and has enjoyed competing in triathlons. She enjoys inspiring others to stay active and lead a healthy, outdoor lifestyle.